1 Planning

So you want kittens?

Responsibilities of having kittens

2 Expecting kittens at home

Pregnancy

Birth

Care for kittens and their mom

3 Orphaned kittens

Feeding orphaned kittens

Orphaned kitten's health

Care for orphaned kittens

4 Adopting kittens

Best age and numbers

Male or female kittens?

Spaying and neutering

5 Making your kitten comfortable

Preparation before homecoming

Safe home for kittens

The first days

Introducing a kittens to a dog or another cat

6 Kitten hygiene

How do you train a kitten to use the litter box?

More to kittens hygiene

Is it necessary to clip kitten claws?

7 All about older kitten's diet

What older kittens need

Canned food vs. dry food

How to choose the right food?

What older kittens drink?

Treats

8 Kitten health

The importance of play time

Health issues

Upper respiratory disease

Infectious diseases

External parasites

Internal Parasites

9 Kitten behaviour and training

Understanding kitten behaviour

Unfavourable behaviours in older kittens

Kitten training

Disclaimer

1 Planning

So you want kittens?

Everybody loves kittens! They are adorable, soft and fluffy, adventurous and playful. They are irresistible, but is a kitten the right choice for you? Even long-time cat owners sometimes forget that having a kitten in the house is much like inviting a toddler to live with you. If serenity is your lifestyle, you will be better off with an older cat. From a kitten's point-of-view everything is created for its enjoyment. Chewing, biting, clawing and climbing are ways with which a kitten learns about its environment. The kitten will be healthier and happier if it has a playmate, so two or more are better than one. There will be less wear and tear on you and your house if your kitten has a friend to chase around. Kittens that enjoy playing with each other quickly learn to control their playful aggression. Bite too hard and you lose your playmate, a valuable lesson and one that you will appreciate when they get their grown-up teeth. Kittens have a way of getting under ones foot and their playful attacks can easily pierce the skin. They learn to retract their claws and to inhibit their biting as they mature but until that time be prepared for scratches and bites. Kittens need more patience as they need to be trained in many different aspects like using the litter box and using the scratch tree. If you have young children, be aware that they can unintentionally suffocate or injure a Kitten if they treat it like a toy. Naturally children want to pick up and hold the living toy. When the kitten squirms to get away, they squeeze harder to keep the kitten in their arms. The kitten may sustain internal injuries and the child may be bitten or scratched.

Kittens grow into cats fairly soon. They are great companions. Many of us live alone and want to have someone around us, someone who loves us, no matter how we look and feel at the moment. Kittens can be great companions for the kids and perfect to teach them the first steps of taking care of others and sharing responsibilities. Once kittens grow into cats they will not need to be around you all the time, so their affection is not overwhelming. Health professionals and researchers are finding that having kittens and cats can actually benefit your health. Studies have shown that there can be reduced risk of cardiovascular and heart disease, reduce stress and anxiety, improvement of your mood and reduced loneliness.

Whatever your reasons are; be aware of the responsibilities too. Kittens are living creatures and your decision is a decision about the life of a living, feeling animal. Such decision should not be done without giving it a thorough thought. Kittens will not stay cute forever and grow into adult cats. So be prepared to follow through with your commitment even into adulthood of kittens.

Responsibilities of having kittens

First of all think seriously about the important step of bringing kittens home. It is much like having a new family member coming home. Adopting kittens for the first time is a lifetime commitment, so it is important to inform yourself first. A good place to start is by understanding that no one can really own a pet. You will own the commitment to care for the kittens and later cats. A commitment to provide their basic needs; a commitment to always provide a home for them; a commitment to return the unconditional love you will receive. Kittens and cats per se are sentient beings and they deserve to be a family member rather than an "accessory." All your family members, if you have a family, need to share the commitment. If you are looking for kittens as an adornment to your home, cuddly toys or short time fun, you definitely should reconsider.

Questions that you should answer yourself before taking the first steps is: Are you alone or are you having a family? If you have a family consider if other family members are willing to share the responsibilities. Does anybody have a cat allergy? How important is your furniture and carpet to you? It is critical that you are willing to make the commitment to provide your kittens with all necessities and to put them ahead of furniture and other inanimate objects till they grow up and are trained to use a scratch pad or their litter box. Stuff happens. Are you willing to live with it? Or will you consider getting rid of them with the first mishap? Will you have enough time to care for them? Can you afford the food, litter, accessories, vet bills for spaying or neutering and vaccinations? Important is to be aware that there is much to be considered in order to give the kittens and yourself a happy and healthy relationship. You can talk to someone you know who had already kittens and can share a bit of their experience with you. It is important to do the homework first before you decide and prepare. There is no returning back once the kittens arrive home. You already show responsibility and the willingness to prepare and learn by reading this book.

2 Expecting kittens at home

Some of you have purchased this book because there are kittens on their way and you want to know how to care for their mom and the kittens.

Pregnancy

The age in which cats can conceive ranges from 4 to 12 months, with the average being 6 to 9 months. Cats are generally about 75% of their mature body weight with 9 months. Cats usually come to heat between January and September depending on the length of daylight. A female cat can be in heat for 3 to 16 days and if she is not mated will come back into heat every 14 to 21 days until she is mated. A cat in heat is very vocal, calling for a male cat, roll on the ground and constantly rub against furniture or your leg. She will assume a breeding posture with her head and front legs near the ground and the rump area held high with her rear legs treading rhythmically. She will spray urine during her heat cycles, be nervously lurking around doors to find her chance to slip outside to meet one of the male cats that are attracted by the pheromones of your cat. Be prepared for noisy nights both inside and outside your house. Cats generally have their kittens 58 to 67 days after mating and there will be from 4 to 8 kittens in each litter. A cat can mate again while she nurses her litter and the average cat could have 3 litters a year. Signs for a pregnant cat are stop of heat cycles, swelling of her nipples, increased appetite, morning sickness (vomiting) and of course the swelling of the abdomen. It is recommended to have your cat examined by your veterinarian to make sure that she is healthy.

Your pregnant cat should continue to have exercise to help maintain her muscle tone and keep from gaining too much weight. She should be on a premium adult food for the first few weeks of pregnancy. Begin adding a premium kitten food to her diet once she is in the fourth week of pregnancy. Each week increase the amount of the kitten food so that she is on all kitten food at the end of pregnancy (approx. week7). Increase the frequency of the daily meals towards week 6. She may need to eat small meals every 3-4 hours as the kittens continue to take up more room. Your cat may eat during the last week of pregnancy and the first 3-4 weeks of lactating, 1½-2 times the amount she ate before pregnancy. Remember that most foetal growth occurs in the last two weeks of pregnancy and lactating will increase her energy needs.

Set up a nesting box lined with multiple layers of clean unscented towels by week 5 of pregnancy, so your cat can become accustomed to it and to avoid that your cat gets her kittens on your bed or in the closet. The nesting box should be large enough for your pregnant cat to have room and easy to step in. Your cat will often choose her own spot and you can place the nesting box at that location. Move the litter box, food and water closer to that location. Cats go usually without troubles through pregnancy. Rare but possible problems can be abortion or towards the end of pregnancy uterine prolapse, where the uterus is pushed out of the body through the vagina and Eclampsia which is a calcium deficiency. Eclamsia symptoms are change in behaviour, restlessness, nervousness, panting, pacing and in its severe stadium as muscle spasms, inability to stand, fever, increase in heart rate, and seizure-like activity without loss of consciousness. There is a higher chance for Eclamsia during nursing of kittens. Your veterinary should be seen in all three cases. Do not give your cat any medication other than the ones prescribed by your veterinary during pregnancy.

Birth

There are a few items that you need to prepare for the birth process. It might be that you miss the birth totally and the kitten arrived overnight or unnoticed but better prepare dry towels and a box for soiled towels. Be sure to wash your hands thoroughly in case you need to give a helping hand.

Your cat will be restless, turn a few times in her nesting box, have rhythmic contractions and get her kittens within one hour after the first labour signs. There might be between 5 and 30 minutes between each arriving kitten. Each kitten is born within its amniotic sac which the mother will remove. She will immediately start to lick the kitten dry to stimulate breathing and chew the umbilical cord off. Help the cat only if she ignores a kitten that is still in her amniotic sac by tearing it gently open and rubbing the kitten gently dry while holding it head down to help fluid draining from lungs and breathing tract. The kittens generally will search for the teats and start nursing on their own. Only interfere if a kitten wanders in a wrong direction and needs longer time to find the teats. Generally it is better to observe and let the cat do what she instinctively does. The overall birthing process can take up to six hours. The cat usually will eat the placentas that come with each kitten. It offers nourishment for the cat but it is better you remove the placentas after she had 2-3 to avoid possible diarrhea or vomiting from overeating them. Remove any stillborn kittens immediately. Observe any excessive bleeding after the last kitten has arrived.

It is important to seek immediate veterinary attention if your cat does not deliver within 1 hour of the first signs of labour or if she expels fewer placentas than kittens or there is excessive bleeding after all kittens are born. Your cat may get Mastitis while she is nursing. Mastitis Is an inflammation and infection of the mammary glands. It might be localized to one gland with no signs of illness. The mammary glands should be checked daily for signs of warmth, pain, or hardness. Milk from each nipple needs to be checked daily for color and consistency. Milk from glands with mastitis may be off-color and clumping. Your cat may have a fever and refuse to allow the kittens to nurse if more than one mammary gland is inflamed.

Care for kittens and their mom

Chilling is one of the most critical dangers to newborn kittens. Make sure that you keep the kittens and their mom in a quiet and warm room. You may need to remove any soiled towels from the nesting box. A healthy kitten is firm, plump, and vigorous. A normal kitten weighs around 100 grams. A kitten's weight should double within the first 14 days of life. Kittens are ok if they nurse about every 1-3 hours until their stomach appear round and they sleep quietly after nursing. Crying and moving a lot are signs that they are not eating enough. The cat will lick the stomach and perineal area to stimulate urination and defecation. She will continue to do this for 2-3 weeks after birth. Kittens will open their eyes when they are 7 days old and they will attempt to stand after 2 weeks. They will start hearing at that age. This is the age where you can introduce them more and more to their environment and get them accustomed to the normal life routines in your household. Spend every day 30-40 minutes handling them to get them used to you. Kittens between 2 and 7 weeks of age can be easily trained to adapt to daily routines.

Kittens will begin at around 3-4 weeks of age to imitate the cat eating and drinking. A secure shallow water and food dish should be available for them. The kittens should receive 3-4 meals a day of wet paste like kitten food. The wet paste consists of dry kitten food blended with water to a paste. The kittens will first check their food and water, walk in it, eat and drink some and get accustomed to more food and less mother milk. They should learn to use the litter box at that time. By the time they are 7-8 weeks old, they should be fully weaned from their mom. As weaning progresses, the amount the mother cat eats should be decreased. Start increasing the amount of regular cat food after the fifth week of lactation so by the time the kittens are weaned at 8 weeks, the cat is on all adult food.

Kittens will begin imitating their mom and showing sand-scratching behaviours. They follow the cat to the litter box and play in it. They learn to eliminate in the litter box by 6 weeks of age. A cake pan with short sides will work at this stage as a litter box. Kittens learn to bury their feces by watching the queen burying hers. Kittens should be vaccinated and spayed/neutered with 6 weeks of age.

3 Orphaned kittens

In such cases the mother cat is not able to adequately care for her kittens. She may not be able to produce milk or she has behavioural or psychological abnormalities which prevent her from adequately caring for her kittens. In rare instances, the mother may actually not be present due to death, injury or complications arising from a difficult birth. Some kittens may be several weeks old before their mother becomes unable to care for them.

Feeding orphaned kittens

Successful care for motherless kittens requires a regular schedule of appropriate feedings, elimination, playing, and sleeping all in a safe and healthy environment. Raising an orphaned litter in the complete absence of a mother is time consuming but rewarding. It is very possible to hand raise an entire litter from birth with the same success rate as could be accomplished by the natural caring mother.

Healthy kittens are plump and firm, warm, quiet, and sleep most of the time. Unhealthy kittens have poor muscle tone, initial high activity levels and cry a lot. If not assisted, they become weak and quiet. Ideally the kittens nurse from the mother in the first 12 hours to allow for ingestion of colostrum, the initial mother's milk during the first day after birth. Kittens are only able to absorb the antibodies from the colostrum for the first 24 hours of life. Orphaned kittens will need to be bottle or tube fed or a foster cat may be found. Foster cats are hard to find but if you have the luck to find one, she will usually accept and nurse kittens that are similar in size to her own. Do not expect her to be able to handle two full litters on her own. Supplementation with a bottle or tube will still be needed but the overall work for you is reduced.

Bottles for kittens are readily available and are the preferred method of feeding. Tube feeding is difficult and less preferred as the tube may be inadvertently passed to the lungs and cause choking when the formula is administered. It might be the only way of feeding if kittens fail to nurse properly. If the kittens are too weak to nurse from a bottle, a veterinarian should be consulted to receive information and a demonstration on tube feeding. Feed a kitten while it is on its belly, not on its back. Commercially prepared kitten milk formulas are readily available and are nutritionally balanced to meet the needs of orphan kittens. Homemade milk formula recipes are also available. This recipe is rather for emergencies if you have no commercial milk replacer handy: Beat three egg yolks in a medium mixing bowl. Add 2/3 cup whole milk and one tablespoon corn oil to the bowl. Add one ml of liquid infant vitamins to the mixture. These vitamins often come in a jar with a medicine dropper attached to the cap. One full dropper is usually one ml although this may vary slightly from one brand to the next. Mix all of the ingredients. The mixture will be a pale yellow color and mostly uniform in texture although the ingredients may separate over time. Fill a baby bottle with the homemade milk replacer and warm the bottle to room temperature in a bowl of hot water before feeding the kittens. DO NOT use microwave to heat! It is not perfectly balanced nutritionally, but will suffice for several days until commercial formulas can be obtained. KMR is a well-known kitten milk replacer. Do not substitute cow's milk or goat's milk for a high quality kitten milk replacer. They are not equivalent. Do not feed raw egg whites or honey to the kittens. Whether using a commercial or homemade formula, only make enough formula for one day of feeding and keep it in the refrigerator. Wash and dry the bottles and nipples or feeding tube thoroughly between feedings. Warm the kitten milk replacer in a pan of water before feeding. Mix well before using to decrease the risk of any hot areas of formula.

The kittens will need to be burped during and after each feeding, similar to human babies. Hold them upright or over your shoulder and pat their back. Bottle or tube feeding needs to be done very carefully to prevent drowning. Substitute 2-3 tube feedings a day (if tube feeding is necessary) with bottle feeding to help satisfy the suckling reflex. This should help decrease the kittens' tendency to suck on each other possibly causing sores.

The first 24-48 hours each kitten needs 1 ml of milk per hour. Each day, increase the amount fed per meal by 0.5 ml until a maximum of 10 ml/meal is reached. Kittens will need 9-12 meals per day. During the second week, they should be on 5-7 ml per feeding. By the third week, they should be started on wet kitten paste which is milk replacer and dry kitten food blended to a paste. It should be given 3 times a day and the bottle feeding continued. By the fourth week, they should receive 4-6 bottle feedings a day plus the paste should be fed 4-5 times a day. The middle of the night feeding can be reduced and then eliminated once they are eating kitten paste well. They can be completely on solid food by 7 weeks of age. Canned high quality kitten food is preferred. Malnutrition is not uncommon in orphans. Speak with your veterinarian regarding the kittens' diet to make sure they develop properly.

Orphaned kitten's health

A newborn kitten is unable to urinate or have a bowel movement on its own. It lacks the necessary muscle control over these functions. A kitten must be stimulated to urinate and defecate. This duty is normally performed by the mother through grooming or licking of the kitten's anal area. Orphaned kittens must be manually stimulated to enable urination and defecation. The kitten must be stimulated after each and every feeding. Fortunately, this is easy. A cotton ball or piece of very soft towelling works well. Moisten it with warm water and gently rub the anal and genital area. Within one to two minutes the kitten will urinate and/or defecate. Some kittens will respond better before eating while others respond better after eating. Try both times to keep the kittens healthiest. Kittens will need to be stimulated in this fashion until their bladder and bowel muscles strengthen, usually by 21 days of age. Most kittens will eliminate on their own by three weeks of age. Observe the urine and feces for signs of ill health. The urine should be a pale yellow or clear. If it is dark yellow or orange, the kitten is not being fed enough. Do not feed more formula at one time but feed more often. The stool should be a pale to dark brown and partially formed. Green stool indicates an infection and too firm of a stool indicates not enough formula. It is possible to feed a kitten too much, but not too often. Too much food causes gas, regurgitation, and sometimes aspiration into the lungs.

To remain healthy, kittens must be kept at the proper room temperature. Young kittens cannot conserve body heat or shiver to create heat. It is very important not to overheat or burn the kittens. Keep a thermometer in the kitten area to monitor the temperature. A simple 25-watt light bulb suspended over one end of a small box usually will supply sufficient heat. Keep a room thermometer under the light source to monitor the temperature. For the first week, air temperature should be maintained at 30° C and a relative humidity of 55-65%. Over the next 3 weeks, decrease the temperature to 24°C. Use common sense. If the kittens are piled on top of each other all the time, they are cold. If the kittens are spread far apart, they are too warm. If they lay next to each other, the temperature is fine. Temperature control is more critical than humidity. Kittens should be kept on a surface with good traction such as a blanket or sheepskin. This will help with development of their motor skills.

Care for orphaned kittens

Orphaned or hand-fed kittens should be raised together to aid in social development. They should be petted, cuddled, and played with for 30-40 minutes a day over and above feeding and cleaning time. Kittens need mental and physical stimulation. If they have littermates, they will stimulate each other when moving. Snuggle with each young kitten as you wake her to eat and for a time after eating. Soft stuffed animals put in the kitten box can offer something to snuggle with while sleeping. It is important for the orphan kittens to have interaction with members of the household at 3-6 weeks of age. Remember, they are still babies and must be handled with care, but you should start to introduce the kittens to noises, grooming procedures, new people, and pets. Early socialization and enabling the kittens to feel secure in their own environment will help prevent many behaviour problems in the future.

4 Adopting kittens

There are different ways to acquire Kittens. Many pet owners have different feelings towards the source for pets. Most will prefer adopting a kitten from an animal shelter. There are Animal shelters full of kittens that need a new home. It is unimaginable when you put yourself in their position how difficult of a situation it is. You certainly will be saving and changing a life for the good by picking your kitten from an animal shelter. Be prepared to choose among many. There are certain things you have to pay attention to when you choose a kitten from the shelter. In selecting a specific kitten, watch how the kittens interact with each other. A kitten should be playful, but not too aggressive. Avoid kittens who hide in the corner or appear to bully their siblings.

Kittens should be confident, inquisitive, and not reluctant to come to you. Kittens who hiss or hide when approached by humans will be much more difficult to raise into friendly cats. The kitten should not cower or show fear when petted on his head. Kittens should readily accept playing with you. Take a string along and drag it on the floor. Well-adjusted and healthy kittens should eagerly pounce on it and want to play. Realize, however, if the kittens have just had a rousing game of tag or wrestling, they may be tired. Kittens are often either very active or sleeping, not much in between. Look for clear eyes, clean slightly moist nose, clean ears, clean and shiny fur, listen for laboured breathing, sneezing or other signs of congestion while breathing. Choose kittens preferably from the same litter as they are already used to each other. If you have to choose them randomly ask to be allowed to observe them more thoroughly. Pay attention to the kitten's behaviours while you handle them. They should be fairly relaxed and not clawing to be put down; they should be playful and interested and not listless. Narrow your choice down to the best two to three or more, whatever your preference is. Observe how they behave when together. Ask for the background of the kittens, their age, why they are the shelter, if they are spayed or neutered, what vaccinations they received. It is important to know what vaccinations are needed and if they need to be spayed or neutered. Rescuing kittens from the animal shelter will give them a new life and they certainly will return your love for it.

If you have a certain breed in mind and can't find the breed you like at an animal shelter you'll probably want to buy from a breeder. When you find a breeder, ask lots of questions. Inquire about seeing the kitten's parents. You should be at least able to see the mother cat. It is possible the father comes from another cattery, so he may not be available. Ask to see littermates if you want to get more than one kitten. Observe how they interact. Ask the breeder why the particular kittens are for sale as a pet if the choice is limited by the breeder. Look for the overall health of the litter. Have a look at the breeders' facilities. Good breeders have an overall well organized and clean facility. Ask the breeder for a certificate of pedigree. You should be able to follow the lineage for several generations back. Good breeders will almost always show their cats and will proudly tell you about their successes. Be sure to get a health guarantee and a contract with terms of sales from the breeder. Ask for, and follow up on references from other happy buyers before making a commitment.

You can find ads for <u>free kittens to good home</u> offered by families that got too many of them or want to find a new home for a cat. Carefully question the family about the kittens and parent cat's history, whether they had vaccinations yet, any illnesses; ask to see the mother cat in the home environment. You'll get a better idea of the conditions the kittens have been living in, whether there is any visible indication of illness in the litter and the condition of the mother cat. Make sure you know if they got any treatments in order to know what treatments you have to organize and pay yourself. Request the proof for treatments, if you are being told that the kittens have been treated, spayed or neutered.

You can acquire kittens from <u>Pet stores</u>. Pet stores usually offer kittens that are already vaccinated. Make sure to get information about the source of the kittens, what vaccination was given and if the kitten is spayed or neutered. Give always preference to pet stores that work with a local animal shelter to give kittens a new home. The advantage of a pet store is that you can pick up the needed supplies right at the pet store and get your questions about cat care answered.

Best age and numbers

Kittens should be at least 8-10 weeks or older when you get them. The crazy playful kitten stage is short-lived. Your kitty looks and acts in many ways like an adult cat after 6 months of age.

For some people the best idea is to by-pass the kitten stage all together and to adopt an adult cat. Many think that older cats cannot adapt to the new home or cannot be trained and choose out of these reasons kittens. It is a misconception because many older cats are already well socialized and have had some good training. Even those who haven't can be very responsive to behaviour training. Kittens need extra attention and training. There is no prefect number of kittens together. There should be at least two, so they can be companions to each other. More than 4 kittens might be too much as they will grow to adult cats and you might overcrowd your home.

Male or female kittens?

The last question to answer is about the sex of the kittens that of course will grow to cats. There really isn't a lot of difference between the sexes character wise, if they are neutered or spayed. Unneutered cats will fight for territory if outdoors, and will liberally spray their strong scent on walls and curtains if indoors, to mark their territory. Females that are not spayed will also spray. Worse yet, they will make themselves and you miserable each time they go into heat by being loud at night and unusually nervous. On the other hand, once spayed, their personalities will be calm. Bottom line is that the sex of the kittens doesn't make a big difference after they are spayed or neutered. If you find several nice kitties, narrow it down to sex. The one thing to remember is that you can avoid big conflicts in your grown up kittens when you keep either only male or female kittens but generally they will get along just fine when the numbers are lower within mixed sexes.

Spaying and neutering

Most kittens should be spayed/neutered between 5 and 8 months of age. To try to control pet overpopulation, many animal shelters spay/neuter all animals before they are adopted. This means they are spaying/neutering animals at a younger age, even 6-14 weeks of age.

Kittens spayed/neutered at a younger age, often have faster recoveries than those spayed/neutered when they are older. There have been no signs of negative effects on the growth rate, behaviour or the health of grown up kittens that were spayed and neutered at an earlier age. Other than population control, there are lots of very good reasons to neuter/spay kittens. Advantages are decreased aggression, decreased spraying and reduced roaming tendency when they grow up. Spaying and neutering kittens is part of your responsibilities towards your kittens and it contributes to avoid overpopulation.

5 Making your kitten comfortable

Preparation before homecoming

There are a number of things to be collected, bought or prepared before you bring your new kitten's home. Do this a few days in advance to minimize stress for you on the homecoming day. Food and water is the most important first thing you need to supply your kittens. If you adopted kittens from others its best to give your new pet whatever food she is accustomed to. If you don't known the backgrounds of your kittens consider purchasing food that is formulated for kittens. Nutrition is being discussed on a later chapter in this book. You may want to purchase smaller amounts in order to be able to switch brands if your kittens do not like the food you provide. Your kittens should have plenty of fresh clean water available.

<u>Food and water bowls</u> are as important as food and water. Although your new kittens can be fed on any shallow ceramic or stainless steel bowls you have in your kitchen, you may want to provide them with their very own dishes to avoid mixing dishes for you and your family with the dishes for the kittens. Plastic dishes are not recommended, as kittens develop a chin rash from plastic. If you prefer ceramic dishes, make sure the glaze is lead-free.

<u>Litter Box and Litter</u> is very important as kittens need to learn how to use the litter box and scratch and cover their feces. Kittens will need a box that's low enough for them to enter easily. A clear flat plastic box that is used to store shirts and sweaters with cuts down for an opening on one side or a shoebox lid will do for kittens.

Plant-based litter seems to be the safest. Clumping clay litter is common, although low quality clay litters tend to stir up dust, which is not healthy to breathe, either for you or your cat. Consider a mat under the box to catch stray litter. You can buy mats for that purpose at a pet store, or buy a few inexpensive carpet samples to place underneath the litter box.

<u>Toys</u> are not necessarily important but might make the transition time to the new home easier for kittens. All kittens love to play, and your bonding time will begin by playing with Kitty and her toys. The

dangling ball or feather kind of toy is a big favourite for interactive play. Catnip mice are another favourite. Kitty houses and climbing trees or simple cardboard houses provide fun and exercise.

A scratching board or stand will start your relationship off right. Your kittys are going to scratch, whether you approve or not. It is better to provide something to scratch on that is approved by you instead of leaving them to have your furniture or carpet as a scratching ground. Some commercially-made scratching posts have catnip scent applied to attract them. Scratching posts covered with sisal are ideal. If your budget is limited, start with a cardboard scratcher.

A cat carrier is a must. Don't try to transport kittens without a cat carrier unless you want to chase after them or lure them from underneath the car seat. A simple cardboard carrier is fine for bringing new kittens home. A large enough cardboard box with many large enough holes for breathing will do for the first transporting too. You will need to replace the cardboard box eventually with a solid-bottomed fibreglass or durable plastic carrier with secure latch and a screened opening the cat can look through. It will make life easy if you need to carry the kittens to the veterinarian or other necessary transporting.

A kitten bed should be provided to give kittens their own sleeping place. It should be not too large and not too small, just big enough so your kittens fit comfortably in when they are together. It should give them enough room to stretch after a nap.

Now you got all necessary things to welcome your kittens to their new home. But there is more preparation needed.

Safe home for kittens

Time to think about kitten's safety in your home. Kittens have a tremendous amount of energy and curiosity. They love to climb into small spaces, jump up onto high shelves and play with objects. They run, leap and pounce on anything that moves. Because of this normal, instinctive behaviour, the average home may contain many hazards for a kitten. Be aware of them and remove or lock away hazards or hazardous material. Store all medications and toxic substances (household cleaners, etc.) in secure cabinets with childproof latches. Toilets with open lids can be hazardous to kittens who may jump up and decide to take a drink. A kitten may fall in and drown. Same is true for bath tubs. Toilet bowl cleaners may leave a poisonous residue, especially the cleaners that are renewed with every flush. Keep fishing line and hooks stored out of reach of cats. Fishing line can bunch up and cut through the intestines if swallowed. Cords for drapery and blinds can cause strangulation. Either tie up the excess cords or cut the loop in the cord. Heat sources such as wood stoves or fireplaces should be screened off. Avoid candles and other open fires. Keep windows and window screens securely fastened and in good repair. Each year many cats fall to death from high risers due to open windows. Keep small objects out of your kitten's reach. Use only safe cat toys; put toys with strings out of your kitten's reach between play sessions. Close the refrigerator or freezer door as soon as you finish taking food out. If you have a second refrigerator or freezer somewhere, make sure that its door is always closed. If it is unused, seal the door shut so that your cat is never able to get into it. Same is valid for the clothe dryer. A kitten might slip inside a still-warm clothes dryer to sleep.

While playing, some kittens will chew on electrical cords, which can cause burns in the mouth, electrical shock, or death by electrocution. Tie up loose electrical cords and keep them out of sight. All chocolate, fudge and other candy, as well as raisins and grapes should be placed out of your kitten's reach. They contain for cats toxic substances. String and yarn hold a fascination for kittens, but if swallowed can lead to serious in the intestines. Keep all thread, yarn, string, etc. out of the reach of curious kittens. Uncooked meat, fish, and poultry can contain disease-causing bacteria. These uncooked foods should not be given to your kitten. Keep your kitten away from the kitchen if possible.

It is important to setup all necessities in advance once you made your home kitten safe and to make sure that the first few hours are calm. Avoid loud welcomes and introduce family members slowly to your kittens so they get used to their new environment.

The first days

There is a huge difference between the first days of kittens and the first days of an older cat in their new home. It is easier to get the kittens accustomed if you are alone and have no other animals at home. Kittens generally need more attention than older cats during their first days. It is best to get Kittens that are 4-5weeks old or older and weaned. There are two important things you can do to get you and your kittens to get familiar with each other. Touching and talking. Touching the kittens not only feels good to you both, it teaches them that contact with you is pleasant, not scary, and self-rewarding. Touching or petting also places your scent on them, so they associate your smell with feelings of well being. This was one of the first sensations they felt when mom licked them and they associate petting with this wonderful safe experience. Studies have shown that handling kittens of even only five minutes increases the kitten's ability to learn. When handling the kittens, be sure to touch their ears, tail, paws, and mouth so the experience is pleasant and routine. Talking is equally important, and teaches the youngsters to listen and pay attention to your voice. The more you speak to your kittens, the better they will learn to understand and react to what you want. That enhances and improves the relationship.

Be prepared for kitten cries during the first few days. Instinct encourages us to go to a kitten when they cry. This is because maternal and paternal behaviour is part of the human social behaviour that would be directed towards an infant. An older kitten can easily learn to manipulate a concerned response from you and could then cry at every desire, from being hungry to wanting attention. In this way, over-dependency on the kitten's part is quickly encouraged. Learn to differentiate between your kittens cries by observing the times and connected reasons. Kittens can cry when they are hungry, seek attention or are in distress. Cries for attention in older kittens can be ignored (the cries will then stop). It is better in the first few days to keep the kittens away in a separate room if you have other animals like an older cat.

Introducing a kittens to a dog or another cat

If you already have a cat it is important to take your cat's personality and activity level into consideration before introducing new kittens otherwise it may cause big problems. Following behaviours have been observed and can give a general guideline how existing cats and newcomer kittens behave.

Existing female cat: Females, in general, are less accepting of newcomers. Male kittens, while more easily dominated by the female, still grow up to be rough teenagers that engage in a style of play that involves pounce and wrestle (not a female's idea of fun). If you introduce a kitten to an existing female cat and she is confident, contented and non-aggressive, there is little danger of her finding a defenceless kitten too. The kitten may even curl up to the female cat and she may become maternal towards the kitten.

Existing male cat: If you have a young male cat, he would really enjoy having male younger buddies who shares his enthusiasm for vigorous play. An older neutered male cat may enjoy "mothering" a kitten, either male or female. They usually make better mother substitutes than spayed females. Males tend to bond with each other unless both have dominant personalities.

It is advisable to allow a meeting of the existing cat and the newcomers with some casual and calm supervision. A nervous or insecure adult cat will initially want to see off the new intruders that are regarded as a potential competitor for food, territory and access to a loving owner. Such a nervous adult cat would need to be put in a cat carrier or crate and with the use of a harness, exposed to the kittens very slowly and carefully over a period of time.

Existing dog: Kittens should be kept away from dogs until they are mature enough, unless the dog is a puppy in which case the introduction can be gradually under supervision. Now how to familiarize kittens to a puppy? You can familiarize them with patience and observation of behaviours on both sides. The puppy should first be contained in a covered crate or indoor kennel in the room where the controlled introduction will be made. Allow the kittens to enter and explore the room in their own time.

Following the initial 15-30 minutes of exposure, and assuming there have been positive signs rather than aggression let the puppy out of the crate. If there was much spitting and snarling, offer the kittens an extended period of 1 hour in the introduction room in which they can calm down.

Kittens and puppies will usually work things out by themselves after the initial contacts but nothing should be forced if there are signs of aggression. Give them enough time and be patient.

6 Kitten hygiene

Cats are naturally clean creatures and dislike "doing their business" where they sleep or eat. They instinctively cover their feces once done. They also appreciate privacy while doing their duty. You can build allegiance to the litter box by positioning it correctly, in a low-traffic area away from the kitten's bed and food bowls. Kittens need to acquire such skills first and may need you to show them what to do if they haven't learned from their mom before you got them.

How do you train a kitten to use the litter box?

Little kittens have tiny bladders and may not have the physical capacity to hold it long enough. Provide a box on each end of the house. A regular size litter box may work well for older kittens but it could be too large for tiny kitties to climb in and out. A disposable cookie sheet or the lid to a cardboard shoebox works until they are bigger. Once older, simply place the familiar shoebox lid inside the bigger litter box to help them transition. Not all cat litter can be used for kittens litter box. The ideal material is fine structured, yet not dusting, absorbs moisture, contains waste and odour and suits the kittens. A scented product that smells nice to you might repel the kittens, so choose something unscented to start with. Wheat-type products or fine clay litters do a decent job of clumping and are digestible should a tiny kitten decide to taste the litter. Most kittens will not do that. Fill the kitten litter box an inch deep with the litter. New kittens won't know where the litter box is. Place the kitten on top of the clean litter, and scratch around with your fingers to prompt imitation. Kittens instinctively copy your behaviour. Even if the kitten doesn't need to "go," a clean box often tempts them to dig a bit, which may lead to the first deposit. Reward the kitten in such case instantly with verbal praise, a toy, or even a tasty treat reserved only for training.

Don't pick your kitties up out of the box. Let them make their own way out of the box and the room, so they will better remember how to get back there the next time nature calls. Leave one recent deposit in the box after they have been productive. The scent draws the kittens back to the proper location and reminds them what to do once there. Make a point of scheduling potty times until you're sure the kitties consistently uses the box. Take the kittens for a pit stop after each nap, meal, and play period, as kittens need to relief themselves more often than adult cats. Remember to keep the litter box clean or the kittens will avoid the dirty toilet and find a better spot.

Clean litter boxes regularly. A dirty litter box often spells disaster. No product will compensate for a clean litter box. See it as part of your homework to clean the litter box often. If you smell it, it's long time overdue to clean it. You might think "of course scented cat litter will cover the smell" but the scent of the cat litter might send your kittens off even in clean form and as a rule of thumb there should be no more than 30% of the cat litter soiled. Most toilet mishaps are caused by dirty cat litter box. Change the litter at least once a week completely. Disinfect the litter box and scoop after each cleaning to avoid spreading and multiplying of bacteria. Use unscented cleaner and disinfectants as a kitten's sense of smell is much stronger than ours and she might be turned away by such scent. Use litter mats to avoid tracking of the litter outside of the litter box. The unpleasant might happen and your kitties might do its business outside of the box. Do not punish them as they are still in training or maybe it might be that your kitten is sick. Check for health issues in such case.

More to kittens hygiene

There is more to kitten's hygiene than relieving and cleaning after themselves. Cats spend up to 50 percent of their awake-time indulging in some form of grooming. Grooming is learned by "copy-cat" behaviour during the first kitten months. Grooming does more than keeping the kittens looking good. It maintains healthy skin by stimulating the production of sebum, an oily secretion produced by sebaceous glands at the base of each hair. Licking spreads sebum over the hair coat to lubricate and waterproof the fur and make it shine. It also removes loose hair and prevents mats while removing dirt and parasites. Grooming is the indicator for a kitten's health. An unthrifty appearance can signal illness. Cats rely on the saliva spread on the fur while dogs pant to cool off. It evaporates to help cool the cat in hot weather. Well groomed fur can be fluffed to allow air circulation against the skin.

Is it necessary to clip kitten claws?

A cat's claws are versatile, multi-purpose tools. Older kittens use their retractable claws every day, for climbing, scratching, pouncing, turning, and balancing. Scratching is part of their regular self-maintenance program to keep their claws nice and sharp for self defence. When kittens scratch, they are actually dislodging and removing a transparent sheath that grows over the claws. Claw trimming is not necessary unless your kitten is scratching more than the scratch tree or board. Trimming your kitten's claws might be the solutions in such cases. Trimming claws is really simple if you approach the task with a prepared kitten. You may have to start off just doing one or two claws a day. Press gently but firmly on the pad area to extend a claw. It isn't necessary to squeeze hard. Do this for a few days to get the kitten used to this before you move on. Examine the claw closely under light to find the pink area in the center (called the quick), once your kitten is comfortable with you handling the paw. The quick is a blood vessel, and will bleed if nicked. Holding the clippers parallel to the flat part of the claw, quickly snip off the tip, being careful not to cut into the quick.

7 All about older kitten's diet

What older kittens need

Cats are obligate carnivores. Simply put, they need to get their protein from meat, not grains. Proteins are made up of amino acids. Meat contains all the amino acids needed by an obligate carnivore. People and dogs are able to get the missing amino acids from other sources, but cats can't. Grains and Vegetables do not have all amino acids that a cat needs. This is why you can't make your cat into a vegetarian. A cat's natural diet is prey such as rodents, lizards, insects, and birds. The prey consists primarily of water, protein and fat, with less than 10% carbohydrate (starch, sugar and fibre) content. Cats are exquisitely adapted to utilize fat and protein for energy. With this in mind the best diet to feed your cat is the diet that most closely mimics the natural prey. When you get your kitten ask the person you get them from what they used as food and let them give you a small amount of the accustomed food with you. Your kitten is ideally already weaned once it arrives at your home. It will be best to continue your kitten on the food she is accustomed to, to avoid the upsets from a quick food change. If you want to increase the quality of the food or change the diet, start by adding a small amount of the new food to her existing food and then gradually increase the amount each day. You will likely find that once your kitten tastes the higher quality food or flavour, she will leave the old food in the bowl. At that point, you can make the switch complete.

Canned food vs. dry food

Feeding <u>canned food</u> is a convenient way to meet your kitten's needs. Canned foods come the closest to mimic the natural diet of a cat. Canned foods are higher in fat and protein, and lower in carbohydrates than dry foods. The high water content in canned food increases the kitten's overall fluid intake, which keeps the kidneys and bladder healthy. The higher fat content in canned foods contributes to skin and coat health. Because the ingredients are more easily digested and utilized by a kitten's body, canned foods produce less solid waste in the litter box. Another important aspect is variety. A hunting cat will eat any small prey she can catch. Likewise, we should feed our kittens a variety of foods. Variety keeps kittens from becoming picky and food-addicted, lessens the chance of dietary excess or deficiency and prevents the development of food intolerances, allergies, and inflammatory bowel disease in older age. It is easy to vary the flavours and protein sources with canned food. Preservatives are necessary to keep canned foods fresh for cats but canned food should not be allowed to remain out for longer time and should be discarded if so.

<u>Dry kitten food</u> is made up mostly from grains because grains are cheaper than meat. The protein percentage of the dry food is labelled higher than on canned food. You have to look at the dry matter basis on the label, which is the accurate way to compare the protein percentage. Canned food has more protein than dry food on a dry matter basis (the moisture removed from canned food). Also remember, as already mentioned before, grains do not contain all amino acids that a cat needs. Grains have a lot of carbohydrates. The carbohydrates in dry kitten food come mostly as starch. A high-starch, low-fat dough is required for proper operation during processing. Cereal grains provide an inexpensive and plentiful source of calories at an affordable price. A few dry foods are substituting with starchy vegetables and soy for cereal grains; but they are still heavily processed and just as dehydrating as regular dry food. Too many Carbohydrates lead to cat obesity with age. The natural diet of a cat contains only three to five percent carbohydrates. Compare this to dry food that contains 35 to 50 percent. Cheap brands contain even more. Dry kitten food is convenient and many leave dry food out in a dish for the kitty to nibble on whenever she wants to. Too many carbohydrates plus too much food leads to overweight cats once kitty is grown up. This problem is becoming an epidemic among cats and only leads to health problems like a diabetic cat. You can avoid this by training your kitties to get accustomed to the right diet and amounts of feed.

Another aspect is that most dry kitten foods are processed with high heat. This will denature (change the structure) proteins in the food. These denatured proteins may cause allergies. Dry food is very dehydrating. Kittens will easily be dehydrated feeding on dry kitten food. Kittens eating only dry food take in only half the moisture of a kitten eating only canned food, even with adequate amounts of drinking water available. Use dry food when you are away for a longer period. Give your kittens only the amount that they can eat in one portion and give your kittens always plenty of fresh water

How to choose the right food?

There are many choices in flavour, nutritional content and price for kitten foods. Kitten food labels are not always giving the full picture of what the food contains. In any case look out for low quality unwanted ingredients like fillers, animal by-products, meat and/or bone meal, animal digest or added sugars. Other ingredients to avoid are chemical preservatives, including BHA, BHT, ethoxyquin, and propyl gallate. Food labels are often confusing and fancy names like gourmet and supreme kitten food might give a better impression than the content would give you.

There are canned foods labelled as natural or organic. Only products with the label of the organic certifier give you the guarantee that the contents are certified organic. Your kitten will eat what she likes and turn the nose on flavours she does not like. She has a good nose for good quality, so it's best to make your own experiences with her choice.

What older kittens drink?

Kittens need enough water to maintain optimum kidney health. Water is essential for helping the kidneys flush out toxics from the blood. Water also helps to keep other organ tissues hydrated and healthy. Cats' body tissues consist of about 67% water, which is naturally approximately the same percentage of water in the prey they catch and eat in the wild. In contrast, dry cat food contains around 10% water, and canned cat food around 78%. Have always fresh clean water available for your kittens, especially if you give them dry foods only. Keep the water bowl for your kitten clean. You might want to avoid scented dish soaps as your kitten's nose is more sensitive than our human nose and can pick up the scent which might make her to avoid drinking water.

How about milk? It is just a myth that older kittens need milk. Kittens don't naturally find milk other than their mom's milk in nature, so their bodies weren't designed to ingest other types of milk. As a matter of fact, milk can cause obesity, diabetes, urinary tract disorders, diarrhea and gas. Kittens are attracted to milk as it reminds them of their mother's milk. The consistency of cat milk is different than cow milk. Cow milk is too high on carbohydrates and the fat is hard to digest. For kittens, milk is not about nutrition; milk is about the carbohydrates, the taste and the memory of the comfort of nursing. Milk is a treat for kittens, but everyone knows that too many treats can't be good. Goat's milk is a better choice as goats milk fat is easier to digest but the carbohydrates are as high as that of cow's milk.

Treats

Kittens all love special treats. Kitten treats are wonderful as rewards for doing the right things, taking medicine, to conceal the medicine itself, for special applications, such as dental for training or for sprinkling on regular food to encourage them to eat. It is recommended kitten treats make up no more than 10% of the total calories they eats. Too many treats increase the calories intake which will cause problems like obesity. Kittens can develop a taste for treats, and they may decide to avoid their own food in favour of the goodies they love. Keep treats novel by offering them no more than two or three times a week. Avoid giving treats when a kitten insists to get treats or begs for treats.

8 Kitten health

The importance of play time

There is a little tiger in every kitten, a solitary predator that needs to exercise its hunting skills on a regular basis. We may have confined this little tiger within four walls, provided it with the finest of foods, but we can't ignore its basic need for hunting. Fortunately, it is not always necessary for the prey to be alive, but it must move. Kittens need exercise like us humans too. Boredom is often at the root of a variety of behaviour problems including aggression with pets as well as people and depression. Two play sessions a day will improve your kitten's attitude, improve fitness and avoid boredom. The play sessions should not stop until the kitten is exhausted, lying on his side and batting at the toy because he is too tired to chase after it. During the session make the toy move as would prey a little mouse or bird. A couple of well-made fishing pole-type toys, mouse toys or balls are good toys for exercising. Other ideas are to stuff cotton socks with cotton balls and catnip, to use old cardboard boxes or just to flash a beam of light on the walls and floor of a dimly-lit room. Keep the exercise session at the same time everyday as kittens love routine. When selecting appropriate toys for your kitten think in terms of what would be safe for a human infant or toddler. Unfortunately, there are no regulations or cautionary statements on toys for pets. It is up to you to determine if the toy is suitable. If it can be swallowed, it will be dangerous. The backward-pointing barbs on a kitten's tongue make it difficult for the kitten to remove items from its mouth. String, yarn, floss, ribbon, twine, rubber bands, bells, etc. can be swallowed and may cause severe injury to your playful kitten. Check toys for glued-on decorations or trim that could come off and be swallowed. For example the small mice made of real fur have eyes that are tacks and should be removed before the toy is given to the kitten.

Health issues

Knowing about the common kitten health problems and the symptoms helps you to detect health problems at an early stage. Catching health problems early will possibly reduce the severity of the problem with early veterinary attention. It will prevent unnecessary hardship for you and your cat. Many cat diseases have the vomiting and diarrhea as symptoms. It is important to know when this might be the sign of a more serious disease and when it is a relatively harmless complication due to bad food or other things your kitten came in contact with. Observe your kitten closely and see if her behaviour and activity is otherwise normal. Think about and try to identify the cause of the problem. Could your kitten have eaten something (like grass or a plant, garbage, or a dead animal) that did upset her digestive system? Watch how your kitten vomits or eliminates so you can describe it to your veterinarian if symptoms persist. Examine the stool or vomit. Collect samples if you believe you will need to take your kitten in. In any case bring your kitten to the veterinarian if there is blood in the vomit, the vomiting is accompanied by diarrhea, the vomit looks and smells like stool, the vomiting is sporadic and there is no relationship to meals, when multiple bouts of vomiting occur over a short period of time, when ingestion of a poison (like antifreeze or fertilizer) is suspected, the vomiting persists more than a day or two, when stomach bloating occurs or your cat tries to vomit but cannot, when there is weight loss and when your cat is showing other signs of illness such as laboured breathing or pain.

Other alarming signs are a bloody diarrhea, diarrhea accompanied by vomiting, fever and other signs of toxicity are present, and when diarrhea persists more than a day or two. In any case contact your veterinarian if you are in doubt. It's better to find out that there is no reason to worry than to catch a disease late and have your cat to undergo more severe treatment.

Following is a list of the most common health problems and their symptoms. Your veterinarian can give you more information and a precise diagnosis.

Upper respiratory disease

Symptoms: Nasal discharge, sneezing, drooling, eye discharge, fever, loss of appetite and depression. Sneezing and eye discharge in cats are the most common characteristics of upper respiratory disease. This is when mouth, nasal passages, sinuses, upper airway, and sometimes the eyes in kittens are affected. There are multiple causes of upper respiratory disease in kittens but 80-90% of the cases are caused by feline herpes-1 (also called feline rhinotracheitis virus) and calicivirus.

Both the rhinotracheitis virus and calicivirus are spread through contact with the discharge from the eyes and nose of an infected cat. This usually occurs through direct cat-to-cat contact, sneezing, food dishes, hands, bedding and other objects which have been contaminated with infected discharge. Prevent further spreading of the aforementioned viruses by keeping the eyes and nasal passages of your kitten clear through regular removal of discharge, increasing the humidity (e.g., placing a vaporizer in the room with the cat) and the possible use of a nasal decongestant prescribed by the veterinarian. Food and water intake may be difficult since the nasal symptoms may not allow the kitten to smell the food, in which case he usually does not eat. Do not force-feed your kitten but encourage it to eat. Keep your kitten quiet and warm, control secondary bacterial infections through thorough hygiene and treat any oral ulcers or eye lesions with appropriate medication.

Because of the contagious nature of the disease, kittens with upper respiratory disease are generally not hospitalized unless their symptoms are severe. In severe cases, fluid therapy, supplemental oxygen or a tube placed in the stomach for feeding kittens who will not eat may be necessary. Most kittens infected with feline rhinotracheitis virus or calicivirus will become chronic carriers of the virus. This means they will continue to be infected with the virus but rarely show any signs of the disease. In the case of rhinotracheitis (herpes-1), kittens will often shed the virus in secretions from the eyes and nose after they have been stressed. Vaccination can prevent upper respiratory disease in cats but its efficiency is not 100%.

Infectious diseases

Infectious diseases in kittens have similar initial symptoms as are also found with many other diseases and always indicate the need for a veterinary examination.

Feline distemper or feline panleuk, as it is often called, is an extremely contagious virus with a high mortality rate, which targets kittens. The feline panleuk virus is extremely hardy and may survive for months and even years. It is easily transmitted through contact, either cat-to-cat, or by human-to-cat. Symptoms are vomiting, diarrhea, depression, appearance of a third eyelid in the inner corner of the eye, rough coat, abdominal pain and a hunched over posture. When born to a mother with feline panleukopenia antibodies, kittens will have a natural immunity for the first eight to ten weeks. After that period, vaccinations should be started. Vaccination before that time is not recommended. The FPV vaccine is often combined in "3-way" shots, which also include protection against feline herpesvirus and feline calicivirus which can cause upper respiratory disease in cats. Kittens receive a series of follow up vaccines and all adult cats should be vaccinated every one to three years, depending on the kind of vaccine used.

<u>Feline Infectious Peritonitis or FIP</u> is a viral disease caused by the feline corona virus that can affect many systems of the body. It is a progressive disease and almost always fatal. Approximately 25-40% of household cats, and up to 95% of cats in multi-cat households are or have been infected. The virus can be found in the saliva and feces of infected cats. Cat-to-cat contact and exposure to feces in litter boxes are the most common modes of infection. Contaminated food or water dishes, bedding and personal clothing may also serve as sources of infection. The virus can live in the environment 3-7 weeks. After 3 weeks, however, the number of virus particles present is probably too small to cause infection. Many disinfectants will kill the virus. Kittens are prone to the disease. Symptoms are weight loss, fever, loss of appetite and lethargy. Anaemia with resultant pale mucous membranes (e.g. gums), constipation, diarrhea and the kitten might be pot-bellied in appearance because of the fluid accumulation in the abdomen, are other symptoms. There is unfortunately no cure for FIP.

<u>Pyometra</u> is an infection of the reproductive tract in female kittens. Unspayed older kittens may develop this severe uterine disease. Bacteria enter the uterus and it becomes filled with pus. The normal 6-inch long, thin horns of the uterus are enlarged to 10 inches long and can become the diameter of a human thumb. Undetected, this condition is almost always fatal. In rare cases, when the condition is

found early, hormonal and antibiotic therapy may be successful. This type of therapy is limited to valuable breeding animals. Generally, the treatment of pyometra requires a difficult and expensive ovariohysterectomy (removal of ovaries and uterus). The toxicities resulting from the infection can strain the kidneys or heart and in some cases may be fatal or cause lifelong problems, even after the infected uterus has been removed.

External parasites

External parasites in kittens can be annoying, such as fleas and ear mites but can also cause some deadly diseases, including Lyme disease, Haemabartonella or Infectious Anaemia. Fortunately, in most cases parasitic infestation can be easily prevented through proper hygiene and sanitation.

<u>Fleas</u> spend most of their time on an animal, but the flea eggs, larvae, and pupae are found in abundance in the environment such as in carpeting, rugs, bedding, and grass. Therefore, a truly effective flea control program always includes treating the environment as well as treating your kitten. Indoor flea control involves mechanically removing all stages of the fleas, killing any remaining adults, and preventing immature forms from developing. Start by vacuuming thoroughly, especially below drapes, under furniture edges and where your kitten sleeps. It is estimated that vacuuming can remove up to 50% of flea eggs. Each time, seal your vacuum bag in a plastic bag and discard it immediately. Use a product that will kill any remaining adult fleas and also stop the development of eggs and larvae. You will need a product that contains both an adulticide and an insect growth regulator (IGR), such as pyriproxyfen or methoprene. Wash your cat's bedding weekly and treat the bed and surrounding area with the same product. Do not forget to also clean and treat any other place where your kitten spends much time. Keep in mind that until all of the fleas in your home have died, you will probably still see some fleas, even on a treated kitten, since some immature forms may continue to develop. Persistence is key in eliminating a flea problem.

At the same time treat the fleas on your kitten or older cat. A flea shampoo as well as a flea and tick spray help to primarily rid the kitten of the fleas she already has on her, although some have residual activity. To properly use a flea shampoo you must be sure to work the shampoo in over the entire body and then leave it on at least 10 minutes before you rinse it off. Sprays eliminate the need of bathing your kitten but you have to be very vigilant and cover every part of your kitten to have the best effectiveness. In both cases remember to protect the eyes and ears. Flea collars can be effective after the initial treatment with the bath or spray but must be applied properly. You should just be able to get two fingers between the collar and your kitten's neck. Be sure to cut off any excess portion of the collar otherwise your kitten may try to chew on the end. Use of oral products, Injections and flea combs are other ways to eliminate fleas. The best flea control is always prevention. Use the flea collar to prevent future infestations.

Ear mites can invade the ear canals of kittens. Ear mites are extremely contagious. They can be passed from the mother cat to her offspring and other animals or passed from other animals to cats. Humans are not affected. Kittens with ear mites will scratch around their ears and/or shake their heads. The ear canals will bleed and either fresh or dried blood will appear inside the canal. If you peer into your kitten's ears you will notice a build-up of a material that looks like coffee grounds. Ear mites are very easy to control. Use just one drop of tea tree oil in each ear and you get rid of the mites overnight. Be careful to not get any of the tea tree oil in the eyes or on the nose of the kitten. You can get tea tree oil in drugstores.

Internal Parasites

Internal parasites are a common problem in cats. Prevalence rates are as high as 45 percent. The parasites can be wormlike or one-celled also called protozoan organisms. The signs associated with internal parasite infections are fairly nonspecific, such as a dull hair coat, coughing, vomiting, diarrhea, mucoid or bloody feces, loss of appetite, pale mucous membranes or a pot-bellied appearance. Common *wormlike intestinal parasites* are tapeworms, roundworms, hookworms and stomach worms.

Roundworms are the most common intestinal parasite of kittens, with an estimated prevalence of 25% to 75%, and higher. Kittens become infected by larvae that are passed through an infected cat's milk. Roundworm infections can potentially become life-threatening if the numbers are so great that intestinal blockage occurs.

Stomach worm infestations are sporadic. Kittens become infected by ingesting the parasite-laden vomit of another cat. Chronic vomiting and loss of appetite along with weight loss and malnutrition may be seen, although some infected cats show no signs of disease.

One celled parasites or protozoan parasites in kittens are Isospora, also known as coccidian, giardia and toxoplasma.

Isospora are microscopic one-celled organisms causing the disease coccidiosis. Virtually all cats become infected with it during their life. Kittens become infected by eating the egg-like cysts that has been passed in the feces and has matured in the soil. The cysts can be infective within six hours after being excreted in the feces. Isospora infections cause significant disease in kittens. The Isospora destroy the lining of the intestine and cause diarrhea. Good sanitation and hygiene will help control coccidia, but accurate diagnosis and effective treatment can only be achieved with your veterinarian's assistance. Isospora of kittens cannot cause disease in humans.

Giardia infections are estimated to be affecting less than 10% of kittens but can be much higher in some environments. Kittens become infected by ingesting Giardia cysts present in the feces of another infected animal, usually a littermate or chronic carrier cat. After ingesting of Giardia cysts, it takes 5 to 16 days before the kitten will show signs of diarrhea. Acute or chronic and continuous or intermittent diarrhea is the most common sign of infection. The majority of Giardia-infected kittens are only carriers of the disease. Careful hygiene will eliminate the risk of accidental ingestion of cysts.

9 Kitten behaviour and training

Understanding kitten behaviour

It is very important to understand your kitten's behaviour and how it differs from human behaviour in order to be able to avoid misbehaving, problems like scratching and to get your kitten to follow certain routines. Many make the mistake to assume that kittens behave mainly like puppies. Puppies follow ranks and you can control their behaviour by being their "top-dog" or if they accept you as the alpha male.

How and when the kitten was handled from birth has a tremendous impact on the development of the kitten and its behaviours too. Kittens who are gently handled multiple times a day and who are exposed to many different people and other animals while they are 2-9 weeks of age are more likely to be friendly and well-adjusted, and generally get along better with people and other animals. If kittens are exposed to vacuum cleaners, kitchen appliances, and other items in the house that are noisy when they are 2-8 weeks of age, they will generally be less fearful of them than those who are not exposed until they are older.

Kittens who did not have a lot of human or other animal contact during this period, or who are mistreated or played with roughly, may be more timid or aggressive. Kittens who do not grow up with their mother or siblings are more likely to have behaviour problems as they grow older. By living as a family, kittens are more subject to frustration and how to properly cope with it. They learn guidelines as to what acceptable behaviour is and what is not. They soon find out that biting and scratching is not tolerated. If hand-reared by people, kittens are less likely to develop inhibitions against these behaviours and are more prone to displaying them.

Cats do not follow ranks like dogs do. Cats establish in their natural habitat an area where they sleep, eat, hunt and mate. They have their home territory that radiates from the home base and its size generally relates to the availability of food. They do not need a large territory unless food is scarce and they have to cover a larger area that provides their food. The cat's territory consists of a network of paths that are patrolled regularly on a fairly fixed schedule. They mark their territory by scratching, spraying, depositing scents through defecating, urinating and rubbing. Cats and kittens have scent glands on multiple places on their body including their faces and feet. On their face, the glands are located around the eyes, below the ears, and on the chin. The scent markings provide other cats with information about the individual cat as well as when she was last there. Scent marks contain molecules called pheromones. Different glands secrete different pheromones which affect a number of behaviours, including reproduction and establishing territory. Marking doesn't repel other cats; it allows a number of cats to share the resources in a territory without ever having to compete directly with one another. For example, one cat may occupy a spot in the morning but leave it for another cat to occupy in the afternoon. This makes it obvious that it is your kitten's natural behaviour to establish her territory at your home too, even at their young age. You can understand now why kittens rub themselves around objects like furniture or your feet and why other cats passing the same object will often stop and sniff, maybe even rubbing their faces on the object to leave their scent as well. Scratching or urinating as a marking habit is certainly an unwanted habit for kittens in the house. As for any habit, it can be corrected by offering alternatives and by training certain habits out of your kitten.

Kittens sleep 2/3's of their life. That means they may sleep up to 16 hours a day and be up at night. There are three types of kitten sleep: the brief nap, the longer light sleep and the deep sleep. A napping kitten is scanning the environment for any small sound. The periods of light sleep and deep sleep alternate. When your kitten settles down for more than a brief nap, she falls first into a light sleep that lasts for about 30 minutes. Then she falls into deep sleep for about 6-7 minutes where her body relaxes and she appears to be dreaming. She will then return to another around 30 minutes of light sleep until she eventually wakes up.

Kittens can hear high frequency sounds we cannot. They can also distinguish the tone or pitch of sounds better than we can. In addition, a cat's ability to locate the source of a sound is highly advanced. These are reasons why a kitten is more sensitive to certain sounds and react stressed to those sounds. One example is the noise of the vacuum that sends your kitten running away hiding. You can use your kitten's excellent ability to hear to your benefit. Please refer to the Training chapter to see how.

Cats are actually very social creatures and can form strong bonds with people and with other animals. Your kitten will show her love in different ways. She might just stare at you and then squint or close her eyes. That is a huge sign of affection in the kitten world. It is to signal to other cats that this cat is not a threat. Lying on her back, exposing her tummy is another sign that your cat trusts you. She is completely vulnerable to you at that time.

Routines and predictable environments are very comforting for kittens, so introduce a schedule and try to keep activities on a schedule. Playtimes, mealtimes and bedtimes should occur at approximately the same time every day. If the household is unusually chaotic due to visitors, the holidays or a planned move, the kittens should be given a room where they can feel safe and secure and where they will have all their necessities (food, water, litter box, favourite toys, a sunny window, etc.) until the chaos is over. Remember that kittens find familiar scents, especially their own or their favourite person's scent very reassuring, so put some of your worn, but not washed, clothes in the room.

Unfavourable behaviours in older kittens

One type of aggression is <u>redirected aggression</u>. Your kitten is playing on the ground, you pass by and suddenly your kitten hisses and claws you. Redirected aggression occurs when a kitten is highly aroused and in an aggressive state (for instance through play or by just having been in a fight with another kitten) and is touched or closely approached by another animal or person. Keep in mind that it is the kitten's playful and predatory nature that enables it to concentrate so single-mindedly on playing. This all-consuming focus of the kitten's attention will blur her judgement of the situation and make her forget that not everything is within her play.

A second type of aggression is the <u>immediate fear induced aggression</u>. Immediate fear induced aggression is resulting from a frightening stressing incident like a loud unfamiliar noise or other sudden changes. Your kitten is in such a case stressed. Stress is described as the mental and physiological changes that occur in an animal when it perceives something potentially threatening. The threat triggers a flood of activity in the animal's portion of the nervous system that controls involuntary body functions such as heart rate, blood distribution, and respiration. The biological changes that occur prepare the animal to either combat or escape the stress causing challenge. Your kitten might be limited in the way it can escape the challenge, so she is forced to combat the stress factor with aggression. Another type of aggression comes from sensitivity to stress factors. Many stress factors over time can make your kitten sensitive and aggressive to even smaller stress factors. The only way to get your kitten back to a normal behaviour is to remove the stress factors.

Play related aggression can show in uncontrollable biting and/or scratching behaviour. While this aggressive kind of behaviour is painful and frustrating to you, try to remember that kittens never do anything without a reason. They are actually very predictable creatures and biting and scratching are cause and effect behaviours just as most undesirable behaviours. There are two basic kinds of biting and scratching behaviours in kittens and both of them are often originally caused by our own human failings. Kittens learn biting and scratching as an important part of their development. The main form of play involves biting and scratching in "winner takes all" battles, whether with another kitten, a toy mouse or a human hand who finds himself in the wrong place at the wrong time. Do not teach your kitten that hands are toys by avoiding agitating playing with your hands. Similar scratching can happen to any other of your body parts that come close to your kitten during play. Do not over stimulate your kitten during play. Stop the playing right away if the kitten starts scratching or biting and walk away, showing your displeasure. Your kitten will understand that this immediate action was related to her biting and scratching.

Scratching furniture or carpet is another behaviour that you might find unfavourable. You already know that in order to feel secure in their home territory, cats routinely patrol the area and mark it by rubbing or scratching. The furniture or the carpet are part of the territory and will be marked through rubbing against or scratching. You being concerned and running to chase your kitten away from the furniture might even encourage the scratching further when it discovers that it gets your attention by scratching the furniture. So a useful territorial habit may turn into an unnecessary nuisance.

Plant eating and soil digging is a nuisance to plant lovers. From your kittens point of view a potted plant is a snack, an entertainment center, and sometimes a litter box, all-in-one. Digging in soil is similar to digging in earth. Sometimes kittens even eat dirt. The reason might be nutritional deficiencies or similar to eating grass to benefit digestion. Eating plants can be related to eating grass too. A good idea is to grow some cat grass for your kitten and cover the soil with pebbles in pots to make digging unpleasant.

Begging for food at the dinner table or treats can be prevented by curbing such behaviour right away. Ignore the begging and if needed push the kitten away to show that such behaviour is not correct. Pay attention to your kittens regular eating and activity behaviour as the begging might be a sign that either it has not enough food or it is just bored and wants attention.

Destructive chewing by kittens not only causes expensive damage to household furniture and other accessories but, in the case of electrical wiring or computer cords, can actually be harmful to kittens. Destructive chewing can be caused by boredom, nutrient deficiency or play. It can be curiosity or teething too.

Kitten training

You can train your kitten by before mentioned routines. Established routines are rarely changed by your kitten unless there are stress factors or health issues. You can train your kitten to lose many undesired behaviours that are not stimulated by stress factors or change in environment. Such behaviours are instinctive behaviours in a for you inappropriate location or learned behaviours. Train your kitten where to use the litter box and change the habit of inappropriate urinating and defecating by feeding the kitten where she is inappropriately eliminating. Many cats will not urinate or defecate in the area in which they are fed. Use upside down carpet runners (the ones with the spikes on the bottom), heavy plastic, aluminum foil or double-sided tape, to limit her access to the area where she inappropriately eliminates. Take your kitten to the litter box frequently, and if she uses it, praise her, or even give her a treat. If you catch your kitten in the act of urinating or defecating outside of the box use a remote correction. This generally means doing something that will startle her without associating you with that action. Tossing a pop can with a few coins inside of it and taped shut toward the cat may get her to stop. Do not punish the kitten. Punishing the kitten, including rubbing her nose in the soiled area will not help. It will probably increase the stress and cause other unfavourable behaviour. In some situations, it may be helpful to confine the kitten to a small room with food, water, toys, bed, and litter box. Once she is using the litter box in the smaller area, gradually allow her into larger areas of the house.

Undesired scratching can be eliminated by training the kitten to use its scratch tree or scratch board. It's as easy to train it to scratch on a proper scratching post. A cat-appealing post should be: 1) at least 30" tall, 2) made of soft wood or wrapped with sisal rope (not carpeting!), 3) mounted in a stable, untippable base. Use some catnip to attract the kitten to the scratch tree or board. Use your own fingers to show the kitten where to scratch and treat your kitten with her most favourite treat if she does the right thing. Do not punish your kitten if she scratches furniture or the carpet but react immediately by pushing her away, showing her that she intruded your territory and get the cats scratch tree, showing her where to scratch instead. Immediate proper calm reacting is important. Praise your kittens for the right behaviour and they will learn through your training a new habit.

There are other behaviours you can train your kitten. Train your kitten not to beg for food at the dinner table by feeding her only at her feeding spot. Never give her treats where you are eating. Train her to not jump on the table or kitchen counter through startling your kitten as mentioned before by throwing a pop can, filled with a few coins and taped shut, toward the kitten. Again, it is important that she does not relate you with the startling action. You can use aluminum foil or double-sided tape to make the exploration on the table or counter unpleasant. Train your kitten to come when you call her by calling her whenever you want to feed her.